SEANNCHAI

[shawn (ek) hee]
The Storyteller

A Compilation of
the Prose and Poetry
of Ronald G. Rogers

By
MICHAEL S. ROGERS

WORDS MATTER
P U B L I S H I N G
OUR WORDS CHANGE THE WORLD

Words Matter Publishing
P.O. Box 1190
Decatur, IL 62525
www.wordsmatterpublishing.com

ISBN 13: 978-1-962467-75-9

Library of Congress Catalog Card Number: 9781962467759

DEDICATION

For Virgil Rogers, the man who taught us about life, love, strength, poetry . . . and magick. Thanks, Pop.

ACKNOWLEDGMENTS

From Ron G. Rogers:

Thanks to Shannon Waynescott, who lovingly typed up my poems and put them in that manila folder. Oh, and Jack Tilton, my sixth-grade teacher, who impressed upon a child of dubious background a love for the written word. To all my children and grandchildren, whom I love greatly, each of you has inspired me in your own way. And, of course, my son Michael, for all his hard work to make this dream come true.

From Michael S. Rogers:

I am indebted to my publisher, Tammy Corwin, for believing in this project. More than this project, actually. She believed in me enough to give me a platform to bring some light to the world. My wife, too, Carrie Rogers. She was my biggest fan before any of this was possible.

TABLE OF CONTENTS

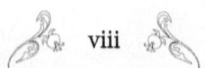

INTRODUCTION

BY MICHAEL S. ROGERS

I was rooting through some old memorabilia one day and stumbled upon it. An old manila folder, creases in the tab, and coffee stains on both sides. In blue ball-point pen across the front, it simply said, "Ron." I thought I knew the owner and yet felt for a moment as if by opening the folder, I was intruding upon a stranger.

Maybe he would prefer to remain unknown.

I hesitated, but could not resist. Before succumbing to temptation, though, I made a vow. I would look into the contents of this folder as if I didn't know the owner. I would explore the contents without expectation, without judgment, without preconceived notions. Whoever owned this folder deserved to be discovered, not discriminated against nor dismissed.

Still, I hesitated. Thumbing the tab back and forth, I let the cover swing up from the bed of manuscripts hidden there, hover over them like a bird riding thermals, drift back

to its place like an autumn leaf freed from her tree. Once, twice; third time is a charm…

Charm. Yes. This folder was a charm against the world. A chance to reveal a poet, a person, to become one in mind and heart with another human being. I desperately wanted to know this person more deeply than he was willing to disclose.

What I found in that beat up manila folder was a man trying to live, learn, and love; but hampered by the pain, bullied by memories, straddled with a fierce loneliness that could not allow the intimacy he so desperately craved. He hid, sometimes, behind a name that calls to mind the Irish in him: Dannon MacLir—or oftentimes, DANNON MACLIR, as if it must be shouted to be heard. Others he left his own name as if to subtly point to his need to be known.

Prose is littered in the poetry, but everyone knows the best writer has a poet inside and the best Poet, a writer. Don't be alarmed, be intrigued. Don't skip one for the other or you'll come away with a picture incomplete. Instead, see what is left there in blood and ink:

TEAGHLACH [chye-lukh] -- FAMILY would love and leave him, show him the world and show him the door, mark him and mock him.

BEATHA [BAA-ha] -- LIFE would comfort and scold him. Teach him, train him, take a toll on him.

LEANNAIN [lee-AN-an] -- LOVERS would elude him. Find him. Honor him. Dishonor him.

DRAIOCHTA [tree- OH (kh) – tah] -- MAGICK would define him and then leave him bereft.

SEANNCHAI [shawn (ek) hee] -- Storyteller. Fate made him that. All he experienced—his errors and injuries, his triumphs and travesties, his goodness and evil—were fodder for this little, old, trampled manila folder that revealed in stark truth what no one else knows.

I know the man. He is my father—and he is all I thought he was, both good and bad. But he is not what he seems.

Perhaps, before we unveil the rest, we should let him set the stage…

Monday, February 10, 2003

This moment begins the first writing practice in this notebook.

. . . This moment begins another attempt at bleeding the source and reason of my discontent.

. . . This moment is a wild writing time that could not exist in the sanity of my normal world.

. . . This moment is the moment to return to chasing rainbows down the well-worn path of my imagination.

. . . This moment is a moment in time that I have somehow lost or forgotten and I just want it back.

. . . This moment I can let it go and make it real once again. All the talent that lies within can explode into my world, my dreams, my magick.

. . . This moment is a love fest that I am sharing with myself, one that has been hidden under the moss-covered rock in a deep and distant fen.

. . . This moment is one that I should take pains to never forget, just as I should never have forgotten how great it is to learn, how great it is to be in class and relate to those around me and to realize once again that I am immeasurably smarter than I ever give myself credit for but also amazingly more ignorant than I could ever imagine.

. . . This moment is for Socrates and Plato and Walt Whitman and W. B. Yeats and Michael Collins and Brian Boru and Bob Hope and Seamus Heaney and Van Morrison and Clannad and the Irish and the Welsh and the Scots, Celtic warriors doing battle mostly within the innermost workings of their minds (with a few physical lessons now and again).

... This moment I've taken a small breath and slowed down just so that I can collect my thoughts (although I'm still writing at a fairly breakneck pace) because it's hard to just keep slamming words onto a piece of paper with any coherency. But ...

... This moment in time has me writing unabashedly for the first time in a long time. It is a beginning of sorts. Good.

PART ONE

TEAGHLACH (FAMILY)

Family is a tricky thing nowadays. Divorce, unmarried partners, kids from different marriages—what we once considered family can become fractured and, at times, permanently dissolved.

So family becomes something greater as it becomes lesser. Who we consider family becomes more about what we experience with them. Too much bad severs, so much good cements. My father's idea of family was shaped by his experiences. He was great at it with those around him, but sometimes struggled most with those nearest him.

His relationship with some of his children suffered, but he picked up children along the way—those he coached, befriended, mentored, and loved. One of my best friends, Chuck Bishop, became like a son; his perspective sheds light on Pop's concept of family.

FAMILY, by Charles J. Bishop II

In my early years, I rarely experienced overt expressions of love. The only visible displays of affection were the hugs exchanged with my grandparents each time we parted, and the gentle morning kisses shared between my parents before my dad headed off to work. To my recollection, this tenderness was not extended to us children. The words "I love you" were sparingly voiced, typically reserved for momentous occasions and instances of parental pride.

I felt uncomfortable when I first saw Ron kiss his grown son. I was stunned when I heard him express love at the end of each phone call or when family members departed. Even when he was angry or disappointed, he expressed his love to emphasize that despite the conflict, he still cared for them.

These open displays confused me. Hadn't Ron just told them a few hours ago that he loved them, and now he's repeating it? Ron and I have had many discussions over the years, many of which have been on this topic, especially since my children started coming into this world.

Not much has changed in terms of my relationship with my parents. Displays of affection are still rare. However, the valuable lessons I've gleaned from Ron have equipped me to foster loving and affectionate relationships with my children, stepchildren, and even my in-law children.

The warmth of those heartfelt hugs, the sweetness of those loving kisses, and the profound significance of saying and hearing "I love you" are experiences that would have been absent from my life if it weren't for the insights and heartfelt conversations I shared with Ron.

Pops, I want to express my deep love for you and extend my heartfelt gratitude. Thank you for everything.

February 1, 2005

> "Rest you here, enchanter,
> While the light fades.
> Home is here, and familiar things;
> A cup, a wooden bowl, a blanket,
> Prayer, a gift for the God, and sleep.
> (And music, says the harp,
> And music)."
>
> —MARY STEWART

These lines I would like to have engraven on my stone when I die. I think that time draws nigh. It's been a good run, mostly into the sun, but the wind in the trees in the shadowy night has been just (even more?) beautiful. For the first time in a long time I feel the mystic calling to me. I've been empty without it. Mayhap my penance is at an end; perhaps the gods have taken the time to look down and say "we have exacted punishment enough from this mortal child that we had such high expectation. Let us give him back his soul and bless him for a while."

I had another TIA today, (mini-stroke, for those in Yorba Linda). I'm weak, tired; but, strangely enough, calm, contained, and content. My darling Jeni is coming to take me to the emergency room in a while. I talked to Mikey on the phone and almost didn't tell him because he is sick with pneumonia, and I didn't want to burden him. But I did and I'm glad I did. It's not something that I should spring on them (my babies). I'll call Tina & Lil Red tonight.

I have been blessed, my beautiful children and so many friends that I hardly deserve,

> "And if on some somber, cloudy day
> While walking, your mind on me should bend,
> Think not of me with grief & sorrow,
> Remember me, I am the wind."

FREEDOM'S CHILD

(FOR MAIRE)

Innocents beguiled;
Waning wintery sun
Casts its constant chill
On ceaseless questing heart.
Bloody blades of freedom,
In desperate need,
Seek the light
As they push up in naked truth
Through moist Mother Earth
And resound in anger
On minds of stone.

Memory blurs, thoughts fray;
Aspiration,
Battered and benumbed,
Dwindles in sea of grey.
Cold wings of reality
Fill heaving breast

With knives of bitterness;
Toll exacted by those
Iniquitous and intolerant;
Bleeders of the wild heart.

She flies in rainbow colors
Soaring
Only to be beaten down,
Once again,
By friend and foe alike.
Souls of stony silence
Steal the summer wind
From beneath her wings;
Running forever into the rain,
Wishing only for the sun.

—DANNON MACLIR

LESSON 1

I offer up
To anyone
Qualities of
Friendship,
Honor,
Love,
And trust.

I ask
Nothing
In return
But
Respect;
Inveterate
And elusive,
Essential
To any
Relationship
That lasts

Into,
And past,
The darkness
Of the night.

—Dannon Maclir

FRIENDS

We stumble through corridors
                  of darkness
And look for some infinitesimal
                  ray,
some small essence
                  of meaning,
to our nebulous existence.
It is but a short time
                  from birth to earth,
Womb to tomb,
                  And we wander
In our blindness
                  And die,
For lack of beauty.
I am a poet
                  And, with my verse,
I will be your eyes
And give to you,
                  My friend,
The beauties of the world.
                  —DANNON MACLIR

BITTERSWEET, THE NIGHT

The sound of the city
Whispers
As it stumbles into the night.
Tires on the street sing,
Advance and retreat,
As cars, buses and taxis,
Weave their way
Through yellow, green, and red,
Then recede
Leaving only echoes of quiet.

Tap, tap, tap
A blind man's cane;
Red and white,
Colors never seen
But known and needed
To circumnavigate
The slang and disharmony
Of the urban scream.
Senses filled,
He breathes the vagrant stench.

Out of place,
The sound of small, bare, dirty feet
Slap dismally their filthy lament
On concrete avenues of grey.
Large brown eyes
Stare into empty silence
To devour the light
From a broken street lamp,
Lost in silent tears.

APRIL, COME SHE WILL

(FOR RHIANNON)

The winds blow cold and chill
Filling the silent, somber, night
With thoughts of winter,
Spring and summer, distant memories;
Autumn, once more,
Heralds the death
Of all.

Rainbow child weeps
As icy fingers whistle
Through torn and tattered rags.
She cries,
And prays.
But no one's home.

I'm
sorry
Rainbow
Child

—Dannon Maclir

The Autumn winds blow chilly and cold;
September, I'll remember
A love once new
Has now grown old.

—Paul Simon

CHILD OF GOD, DO NOT WEEP: RHIANNON

The winds of time
Blow dust and falling leaves
Down narrow paths
Then silently, they die.

Loneliness of empty places
Of leaves' impressions,
Touched by just that flit and swirl,
While shadows grey fell earth and sky.

The solitude of once-lived world, now dead
The winds of death heap tawdry trash
Upon the last Rainbow Child,
And from the depths of anguished heart, a cry.

Do not weep, Rainbow Child,
Do not weep, do not weep;
I will hold you to my breast
Until you sleep,
Until you sleep.

—Dannon Maclir

DREAMER

Rheumy eyes, care-worn face,
Speechless, sightless, staring inward.
As I stare into the eyes
Of this aged and ageless man,
A tear
Rolls silently down
His lined and sallow cheek.
He does not blink,
Nor does he acknowledge me
In any way,
But continues to stare inward;
Age etched into every line.
And he, lacking the means
To communicate his pain,
Relives those memories of gentler times.
Christmas, and his children laughing;
Easter and each of them dressed,
Little ladies and gentlemen,
Then on to church
To thank God for His sacrifice,

His bountiful love,
And eternal blessing.
Memories of lost love
And broken hearts;
Of beautiful city girls
With sleepy summer smiles.
And that one special lady
Who entered his heart,
Who remains there,
And always will.

Sweet memories,
Now become bittersweet,
As he faces the Autumn of his years.
And as I watch the tear
Complete its weary path and die,
I know that deep within an old man's mind
    is a young man who dreams.

OLD MAN

DECEMBER 21, 1979. I walked into the room, slamming the door behind me. He sat there at the kitchen table in an old faded white T-shirt, belly hanging over a pair of nondescript grey trousers. He greeted me with the smile, with just the proper amount of upper lip drawn back to give a hint of arrogance and disdain. It was probably mirrored in my own smile; he had taught me well.

With that cocky grin and a shuffle of the cards, he challenged me, "Are you ready for your lesson?" and I laughed. "As I remember, the last time we played I was the one giving lessons." He laughed, too. "It was luck. Besides, I took it easy on you. It's been a long time since you had won. I surely don't want you to go around cryin' about how bad your old man treated you when you came to visit."

I walked over to the stove and turned the burner on, then went to the sink, filled up the sauce pan he used to boil his coffee water in, and doled out a heaping teaspoon of Folgers Instant Coffee. I put a like quantity in my own cup and sat down, sliding his cup over to him.

He shuffled the cards again, then dealt. Three to me, three to him, three more to me, and the final three to himself, he then turned one up. It was the Ace of Spades. I looked at him and he gave me his best sneer.

"What are you doing?" he said. I looked at the cards in my hand. I had the queen, nine, and five of spades, the ten of clubs and king and five of hearts. I gave him back sneer for sneer and led the five of hearts. He took it then with the ten of hearts and already had me for ten points on game—but I had successfully maneuvered him into the lead. He sat there for a moment, not looking at the cards but looking at me. Smiling again, he led the ace of hearts. I could either play my king, which would give him seven more points for game or I could trump his ace, which would give him the advantage of putting me back into the lead. I took the ace with the nine of spades and then led back with the queen.

I heard him curse under his breath as he threw the ten of spades onto the table. I wasn't fooled for a moment. It was the king of spades. He was holding it on me and I knew it. I just couldn't figure out why. What the hell, too late to worry about it; just have to play them and let them fall. I led the king of hearts and he threw off the trey of clubs. I now had nineteen points for the game to his ten, but I still was sure he was holding the king on me.

I led the five of spades to draw him out. With a certain relish, he played the jack of spades and, with a twinkle in his eye said, "Jack!" He led the King, as I knew he would, and took my last card, the ten of clubs, which gave him game.

"High, Jack, and the game! This shouldn't take long at all." He was absolutely right. The final score: old man 11, pupil 3. It had taken him just four hands.

He got up and fixed us another cup of coffee. He started to bring them over to the table when he suddenly broke out in a paroxysm of hacking and coughing. He sat the coffee down, spilling it on the oilcloth that covered the table. He stood there, leaning on the edge of the table for support, his breath coming in short, staccato-like bursts. I asked him, "Are you all right, or are you just trying to get out of playing the next game?" He laughed weakly and said, "I guess I'll have to hoist the white flag. I'm feeling a little piqued."

DECEMBER 24, 1989. It snowed this Christmas. It's been ten years; sometimes it seems like it's been twenty, but tonight it seems like yestereve. Christmas Eve. It's seven below zero outside, and I know that the Old Man is feeling the cold. It's crazy. It's three in the morning and seven below, but I have to go see the old man. He's counting on me.

DECEMBER 21, 1979. "Wait a minute, no excuses. You can't beat up on me that bad and run out on me. Sit down here and take your medicine." He just kept on walking through the bedroom and into the living room, where he sat down in the old, dilapidated, stuffed chair that he loved so well. It wasn't until then that I realized that he really was sick. I followed him in and sat down on the edge of the sofa. He looked at me, the devils back in his old Irish eyes, but underlying that, something else. For the first time in my life, I saw mortality staring back at me through my old man's eyes.

"I don't feel well, son, and haven't for quite some time. I should probably check into the hospital, but it's only three days to Christmas, and I want to see my grandchildren open their presents on Christmas morn. I don't think that's too much to ask, do you?"

"No, Poppa. They love you and would be heartbroken if they couldn't see their Grandpa on Christmas."

DECEMBER 24, 1989. I'm glad that I have a new car on a night like this. It's fit for neither man nor beast out in this cold. The heater won't start warming up until I reach New Salisbury and won't really be warm until I make it to the outskirts of Georgetown. It's not important. The old man is by himself tonight; he needs my company because I don't think anyone else will go visit him on such a cold night.

DECEMBER 21, 1979. "What's wrong with you, Pop?" I asked him. "I'm just having more and more trouble breathing. Sometimes at night, I almost suffocate trying to catch my breath." He blew his nose, and it seemed as if his color was a little better and that he was breathing easier. After another moment, he was himself again.

"You want to finish your lesson?" he asked. I said... I said, "Sure." So we went back into the kitchen. It was his day; I didn't win a game.

When I got up to go, I made him promise me that if he got to feeling too bad he would call me and let me know so that I could take him to the doctor. "Doctor?" he said as if it left a bad taste in his mouth. He gave me the grin again and said, "Go on, get the hell outta here."

DECEMBER 24, 1989. The Charlestown Road exit. Almost there. Even with the heater blowing I can still feel the cold seep in from the winter night. Ten years is a long time and I guess everyone has pretty much forgotten. But I haven't. There's the gate, just a few more minutes. Ten years...

DECEMBER 24, 1979. The noise woke me. For a minute I thought that a car had ran into the side of the house and I bolted upright. I yelled out, "Is everyone okay?" I heard Dad from the other room say, "Yeah, I just went to sleep and fell over and hit my head on the coffee table."

I got up and went into the living room. He was just starting to get up off the floor when he attempted to say something. His words came out garbled and he fell back on the floor. My mind screamed *Stroke! He's having a stroke!* but I can't do anything about it. I grabbed him from behind and held him yelling for mom to come in, quick. When she did, I told her to call the EMS. She was crying and hysterical but still managed to make the call. I could feel the tears running down my face as I repeated over and over, "Daddy don't die, please don't die."

Somewhere in my mind I heard a little boy as if from a great distance, begging his daddy not to die. I suddenly realized that the voice of that little boy was my own.

DECEMBER 24, 1989. It's always easy to spot the place because of that one big evergreen that stands behind and to the left. The snow gives it a ghostly beauty as I pull to a stop. I haven't been to see him in so long, not since the last time Mikey and I were here. Poppa always likes it when his grandkids come to see him. I wish they were with me now.

JANUARY 8, 1980. He'd been laying there in intensive care now since they brought him to the hospital. In the background I could here the muted sound of *We Wish You a Merry Christmas* coming from the radio in a patient's room down the hall. He lay there so still. The doctor came out and asked to speak to me. It had been fifteen days. No movement, unable to breathe without the life-support system. I spoke roughly to the doctor, "Is he always going to be like this?"

I could see it in his eyes. He wanted to tell me anything but the truth, but I wasn't going to make it easy for him. Finally, he just shrugged his shoulders and looked away. "What happens if you take him off the life support system?" "He may last for three or four hours," was his reply. I thought of him, and for some reason I remembered him singing to me when I was a child, *When Irish Eyes Are Smilin'*. I knew he would like to sing that song again. "Take him off."

He died three and a half hours later, just a little after midnight: January 9, 1980.

DECEMBER 24, 1989. It is unbelievably cold. The wind chill factor on the weather forecast is forty-one degrees below zero. I left the car running and I picked up the wreath, carrying it in one hand as I turned my collar to the cold. The wind whistled loudly as my footsteps crunched on the snow. The numbness that I felt earlier is gone. It's Christmas Eve, and I'm almost there.

The tall pine guides me true and I'm standing in front of where my old man is resting. He knows I'm here as I brush the snow away from his stone. The tears streaming down my face have already turned to ice but I neither feel them nor care. It's Christmas Eve and I'm with my Daddy. Merry Christmas, Poppa.

EPITAPH
or
DAVID

Behold the pale rider
Come too soon;
Flagrant disharmony
Passing pale hand
Over unsuspecting souls.
And one,
Wracked with pain
And anguish,
Casts gauntlet down
To challenge
That last good night
And dare the Reaper.

Gunfire breaks down
Barriers
Of deadly darkness.

SEANNCHAI

Deadly missile
Creates havoc;
Creates scarlet patterns
Of life,
Leaking away, then silence,
And sounds of the city.
To kiss the night
And fleeting soul
To final rest.

ELEGY

Dreams like clouds of morning mist
Dissipate in the too light of day.
Give me the night and the wind,
Into the mystic to dance and play.

And if by some chance of fate
The wind beneath my wings should die,
Do not suffer me to remain earthly bound,
For as the wind goes, so do I.

And if on some somber cloudy day
While walking, your mind on me should bend,
Think not of me with grief and sorrow.
Remember me; I am the wind.

Tuesday, February 11, 2003. Amber's Birthday. She's 27.

Of course . . .

The writing yesterday, the first, or the start, of the re-booting of my attempt to write something significant, was an unleashing of the wild heart. This writing, while being much more subdued, is no less a pursuit into the winds of thought that circle through my mind:

> Some of us,
>> The dreamers,
>>> Were born to dance upon the wind.

I wrote this on every notebook, every folder, everything, that I carried when I was in school. When I quit going I effectively strangled myself intellectually, spiritually, morally, and creatively. I have been empty, unable to write even bad poetry. So now I have gone back to basics. To write every day, to put some words on paper, and to open those doors once more into the recesses of my mind. I have stories, I have poetry, I have at least two or three good books. Maybe more. Natalie Goldberg's first exercise in one of her first chapters of her book, *Writing Down the Bones,* is to describe the light filtering through a window. I get this vivid picture from a line of a Paul Simon song:

It's a still life watercolor
Of a now late afternoon
As sun shines through the curtain lace
And shadows wash the room.

—SIMON & GARFUNKEL

When I think of light through a window this is what I see. It's cold outside. I'm sitting in a Jerry's Restaurant, a place I've sat before, waiting to leave. I worked on the road in the mid-1980's and it was from here that we always took our departure. The light through the window then was a light of innocence, an innocence that a man in his late 30's had no right to ever have. I should have already seen the garish neon of disillusion. But in sooth I had not. The arrogance that I had, the knowledge I did not.

PART TWO

BEATHA (LIFE)

The ancient Greek word for life was *zoe*, found often in the Bible and in many other writings. It was used to encompass all of life—the physical, mental, emotional, social, and spiritual elements of a person. The Irish call it *Beatha* and it doesn't surprise me that it almost sounds like a laugh, a guffaw, an amused bomb that goes off in the room, BAA-ha.

But not all life is laughter and not all experiences are good. What shapes us most, the good or the bad? When we think about it, they both have a hand in what becomes of us. Either we accept it as ours, or we rebel against it. And rebellion often sounds like a guffaw.

Pop accepted his experiences and rebelled against them at the same time. I can hear his deep belly laugh at life right now. I've learned to do the same.

Life, by Jeni Belcher.

I remember, when I was a child if I was hurt or angry, I would climb a tree in the woods and entertain the idea that no one would ever find me. Muscle fatigue got the best of me. Or I would take off walking, sometimes barefoot and in a hurry, traipsing through the forest with clenched fists and tight jaw until that feeling dissipated and my angry thoughts were replaced with wonder and adventure.

I would spend hours in the woods making up stories, sometimes being the princess, sometimes being the fierce warrior who slayed dragons and bad guys. Sometimes, stories were about other people, imagining the romance of an elderly couple who once inhabited the old shed down the hill, love lost to the tragedy of older age and inevitable death.

There was a creek at the bottom of the hill that housed a flat rock outcropping large enough for my teenage body to find root, and there I would sit and attempt to meditate for the first time, just like the gurus in India that I had read about in the Bhagavad Gita.

30 years later, I still run to the woods when things get hard. I still look for a creek bed or a hollowed-out tree in which to root myself and breathe deep until I find calm again. I still meditate. I still think the Bhagavad Gita is one of the coolest books I have ever read.

My dad loves books. Not just prose and poetry; he loves the physicality of books. I remember, as a child, books strewn everywhere. They were part of the landscape. They made home feel like, well, home. My passion for poetry sparked early, beginning with Shel Silverstein. As the humor of childhood transitioned to the seriousness of adolescence, I found the Romantics and the Beats resonated more, and I went into the world each day wearing my Bohemian armor, always carrying a book of poetry. As Paul Simon said, "I (had) my books and my poetry to protect me." I still hold books in this regard, not just stories but physical barriers between me and a world that can be too heavy sometimes.

These are the things my dad taught me that shaped how I live my life. Go to the woods as much as you can. The woods will bring solace. And carry a book wherever you go. You never know when you'll need it.

March 3, 2003

> . . . I remember, I remember,
> The house where I was born.
> The way the sunlight came creeping
> Through the curtains in morn.
> It never came a bit too soon
> Nor brought too long a day,
> But sometimes I wish that friendly sun
> Had borne my breath away . . .

This poem, the author, who eludes me at the moment, is a poem from my seventh grade teacher. I did not know then that, once the façade of innocence was removed from my eyes, that I would be so beaten up from the world until I would come to a point when I no longer had anything left, that I would be bereft of everything that I hold dear and so alone that nothing meant anything to me/that everything meant everything to me. Empty. No one.

> . . . I remember . . .
>> Christmas morning . . . I would
>> be four years old in twenty days. I
>> got a/no/my favorite present
>> was the only one I remember . . .

It was a barn with white rail fence. It had (I think) two cows, black and white, chickens, pigs, one horse, brown with

MICHAEL S. ROGERS

black mane and tail. The one friend that I have known longer than any other human being besides my mother, father, Aunt Geri, Uncle Marshall, and my two cousins Kenny and Jack, was Johnny DeMoss. We lived in the same apartment house where the rats owned the night and would run across you in the dead of night. It was a great Christmas and I was happy. It's (this apartment) the only time I remember my mama ever treating me tender beside when I was five and we lived at 1211 N. New Jersey. I had a red tricycle and we lived on the second floor. I remember that I drove with a precision up and down this hall, in and out of the rooms, coming close to the stairs but always in control. Maybe that was the most control I've ever had. We moved.

When I was five, I remember New Jersey Street, one of only two places I have ever lived that I thought of as home. We lived in (or we moved) 56 times from the time I was born until we moved to New Albany in May of my 16th year. We lived for (I think) almost 3 years there. My Dad painted the whole house, put a border up all around the ceiling. I remember him taking me with him when he went down on Massachusetts Street to a carpet place to get a 9X12 linoleum for the kitchen of our house. It was probably ten or twelve blocks there and back, a long walk for a little kid. My father carried that rolled up roll of linoleum on his shoulder all the way home. I do not remember him stopping or putting it down the whole way. It was cold, probably late November, Dad wearing his overcoat and me in a red snowsuit with leggings and sheepskin collar on the upper. God, how I loved my father. He was cynical, sarcastic, laconic, sensitive to a small man-child, a sadness in his eyes that never seemed to leave except when he had that Irish twinkle in his eyes which usually bid bad news to whoever it was that was foolish enough to fuck with him. We took that linoleum home, it was probably 9:00 pm when we got home. He put it down that night.

. . . I remember Dad coming home one evening in summer in a black panel truck driven by a young black man. They pulled up to the curb and Dad got out, went around to the back, and pulled out a large cardboard box to the edge of the truck. The black man had gotten out on the other side. Together they packed the box inside, opened it up, and pulled out this strange contraption that had a glass front that looked like a fogged up window. They plugged a cord that ran from it to an electrical socket and *voila*, it lighted up. There were geometric designs across it but after fooling around with it (my Dad's friend from next door helping) a picture like at the movies came on. A man was telling about the weather and then something else and then they played the *Star Spangled Banner* and all we were getting was fuzz and snow. We were the first on our block to own a T. V. 1952.

In September, 1953, my mom, (who had grown very big around the middle) left in the middle of the night in an ambulance. When she returned in three or four days, she brought back a little baby brother for me. He wasn't there long before he developed a rash and other symptoms that they diagnosed as an allergy. I had a little black dog, a "Heinz 57."

They determined that the baby was allergic to my dog. They didn't get rid of the baby. They did get rid of my dog. I didn't own another dog until I was 36 years old. My Aunt Gen came to live with us to take care of me because my mother was awfully puny after birthing. A short time later, she sprained her ankle, so Aunt Gen stayed longer. She taught me manners, the proper way to use my silverware, and once, when she thought I didn't respond quick enough, she slapped me in the mouth. I'm not sure but I think I was more surprised than hurt. Later when I became an adult she told me many times how much she regretted and was sorry that she had done that. She also told me that it was unbelievable that I had turned out to be such a fine person because no one had ever went through as bad a childhood as I had. I remember that when she said that we were at her trailer right before she passed away. My wife Vinny and my new three month old darling Heather was with me. It brought tears to my eyes because I did not know that anyone else knew or even cared about what those years had done to me. She's gone but I love her because she cared so much for that little dark-haired solemn child that was me.

. . . I remember the day we moved. Something bad had happened. I remember them setting our dining room suite out in the alley and then us leaving. We left a lot of stuff behind. Most of all we left whatever was good or whatever was happy behind. On New Jersey I had a lot of friends. Steve was my best friend. His cousin Floyd was the neighborhood born loser. He always had a pained, whiny expression on his face. There was Faye who they found me with under a wagon (horse drawn, can you believe it) sans all our clothes. What? I don't know. She lived next door. There was Butch next door on the other side who was probably eight or nine but he was like a big brother to me. And there was Sharon who was an old lady, God, she must have been 10 years old and I was totally in love with her.

. . . We moved to Walnut Street. It was almost downtown and there were no kids at all. It was one of the loneliest times of my life. I had started kindergarten on New Jersey but I was in first grade by the time we had moved. I remember almost nothing of it. It was generally exciting. A lot of it was mingled with anxiety, fear, but always with anticipation. Of course it ruined me for any type of sedentary existence when I became an adult. It may be that that is the reason that none of my relationships have stood the test of time. But I have loved and been loved by many people. We once moved from Ogden Street to an apartment on 10th Street, were in there one night and had to move again the next day to an apartment on Broadway . . .

"14"

Neon light, shining bright
Walking city streets at night.
Escape from day, I fade away,
Taking wings in mystic flight.

Each day I flirt with hate and dirt,
Angry stares with visage curt,
I turn within, block out the din
To camouflage the pain and hurt.

But like a sneer the night appears,
Flashing lights that growl and leer
And I become with the night as one
Hard and bad; forget the fear.

Stepping over a broken bowl,
I lash out and kick it with my toe.
The anger grows, the night wind blows,
Hatred in me overflows.

Neon light, shining bright,
I don't really need your light.
The hate will do, will see me through
Walking city streets at night.

SOUL SEARCH

You cry and ache

        in the night,

Spirit torn

        and worn;

From your insistent

        search for light,

And stand forlorn

        for being born,

And wondering…

        WHY?

—DANNON MACLIR

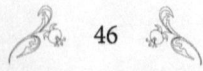

CITY LOOK

Faces talking, sitting, walking,
Standing, leaning, working, cleaning;
Hurrying, ambling, scurrying, scrambling,
Taunting, teasing, never ceasing.
Bankers, brokers, strikers, strokers,
Lovers, fighters, and One-nighters.
Feeling, filling, healing, killing,
Laughing, crying, living, dying;
City faces fill empty places,
Leaving lonely livid traces
Of silent, solitary, single, souls
And eyes filled with tears.

OUTCAST

Treading softly,
Shadows slink from giant oaks
That press in murky darkness;
A spectral thing stalks in subtle silence,
Invisible to all but the denizens of the night.

Cheery warmth
Of flickering shadows
Cast forth their lingering light
From sleepy cottage windows;
Sanctuary.

Hearth and candle proclaim
That within,
The wards of light
Hold at bay
The winter night.

And other things.

Intent gaze, it stares within;
Star-crossed, emotions mixed,
And something else, ill-defined,
But savage
As the wolf.

And slowly then, into the night.

Restless soul, outcast thing,
Tarry not,
The night awaits.
Shadowsong filled with wanderlust
Echoes in the night.

Let the moonlit open road
Fill you with its freedom
As it whispers and calls its exiled souls,
"Come into the wind,
Come home."

SOUL SEARCH II

Give to me

    Surcease from sorrow

An ending to this

    constant pain;

Perhaps,

    For me,
    the road tomorrow

To ease my mind

    with wind and rain.

It always seems

    to come to this

With but short periods

of brief respite;

Autumn sunshine

giving way

Surrounding me

with bitter night.

—DANNON MACLIR

AWAKENING

Twas but a moment,
A second's run,
That made me turn my head.
A fleeting look,
A fleeting thought,
That filled my heart with dread.
For through the window
Of my mind
Like an old lost friend,
Unwhispered words
From solemn eyes
Touched my heart again.

—DANNON MACLIR

THE THINKING PLACE

Look inside the thinking place,
The place where dreams are born.
Search every nook and cranny
From the darkest night till early morn.
Call out the terror, grinding, grim,
As you pursue each missing link.
Stare into the empty void bereft
As spectral thieves stalk and slink;
Then steal from you your words of love
Words of death, and words of life,
Words of emptiness and hate,
Words of weal and words of strife.
They steal from you your inner being,
Pound you, beat you down, until
You reel in punch-drunk attitude
To recapture the touch and feel
Of words that weave their magick spell

SEANNCHAI

Of lines and rhymes and Mother Earth,
Of Sun and Moon and wind and rain—
Sorrow, sadness, joy, and mirth.

Therein

Lies magick.

—DANNON MACLIR

CHANGELING

Street light burning,
Casting shadows in the city night.
Faces turning
To flee or face the Godless sight…

    We gather in the evening gloom
    Fear penetrates our every being.
    Repulsive aberration there; weaving its evil snare.
    Terror at the cost of things unseen
    And in the dark, darkling loom.

    One step; two; down torchlit hall,
    Hammering heart in heaving chest,
    Scarlet that's rife with evil like
    Red door closed at one's behest,
    Seems to beckon, seems to call…

SEANNCHAI

Open door to ebon room
Something shambles in the waiting black
With horrid dread, like one undead,
With grisly totems in unclean sack;
Unholy portent of impending doom.

Now with horror I perceive
A ghastly creature with lurid leer.
Ghoul unconsecrated, who has perpetrated
Loathsome, hideous deeds of fear,
Appalling spells that wend and weave.

And from the darkness of a well
Recognition, as my mind grows numb
And as I draw nearer, my reflection in a mirror
Reveals the man that I've become.
A darkling creature from the pits of hell.

Soul light burning,
Horror stalks the city night.
Faces turn and one face turning
Pale with sacrilegious light.

—DANNON MACLIR

R. I. P.

He sat there while the rock 'n roll
Pounded in his brain.
He took another drink of beer
Listening to the last refrain.
It burned into his inner being,
The lyrics cut him like a knife;
It was a song of love long lost
And of a man who had been tossed
Into the hell that held no life.

Far from being sad,
The music brought him up
As it almost always did,
Filling up his cup,
Overflowing, bathing him.
The music sometimes made him smile
And even through the agony
He could drown the blasphemy
Of the pain for a little while.

Shadowed memories, faded now,
Negative prints of bleak despair—
Listening to Beck's hot white boy blues,
He opened another can of beer.
Lightning flashes, slide guitar,
"Jeff's Blues" filling up the night,
Shutting out that horrid glimpse
Of all the bastard hellish imps
That followed him into the light.

The Strat hit a high, screeching chord,
Black cat stalking black cat's lair,
Kicking, biting, snarling, fighting
As they tumbled down the stair.
Then away, one slinking softly,
Taking with it the hurts and wrongs
And he, in blinding revelation,
Finally gained a measure of salvation
in Rock' n Roll and hot blues songs.

EMPTY

Words trickle__
All but dried up__
Like the back streets of my mind.
The poetry is lost__
With whatever spiritual essence
That I may have had.
Empty__
A word
That looks
And sounds
Like exactly what it means__

The empty vessel
That I've become
Now fills with only fear__
A poor substitute for faith.
Priest and Poet__
Friend and foe__
Companions and acquaintances
Advise and admonish,

Browbeat and berate,
That which is I
Into a belated attempt
At new faith.

And I balk__
Procrastinate until the hour grows
Late.
Then wielding my fear
Like Excalibur
I dare and defy
The fates
To defeat me if they can.
Knowing all along
That my mortality
Leaves me bare
To the inevitable.

PRAYERS

Sunday morning, city sounds,
Play measured cadence in my mind.
Kitten climbing, church bells chiming,
Love bird singing just behind.
Sidewalk silence, sunshine stealing,
Overflowing streets of grey.
I sit alone, all on my own,
And thank God
for the lovely day.

UP AND DOWN

We go out into the night to bounce off, each and every one, our attempt to touch, if only for the miniscule moment when gazing into another's eyes across a crowded room, a chance to invoke that intimacy and tenderness that we cannot live without. We live within ourselves, with heartfelt prayers that we may live within the heart and soul of someone else. Some are fortunate on given night. Fate plays for them a winning card and, for once, the journey home is not alone or in vain. This endless search up and down a lifetime becomes, as we age and lose ourselves in reality, a study in desperation. Do not weep to feel and see life move on its inexorable way with no return upon your investment. Take what is offered willingly and embrace those that remember to spare their valuable time to invest in you in return. Give more than you receive. This, in the long run, will fill and fulfill you much more than the taking. Only loving up and down a lifetime makes a lifetime worth the while.

Ask me again in the morning and I'll try to fill you
up and make you smile.

—Dannon Maclir

RAIN

The hills are still dormant
Only a touch of spring,
        A few green buds,
To show that the cycle of life
        Once again has begun.
           The wind beating it to a froth.
As the grey clouds bring with them a cold, chilling
rain,
    It soaks the ground and my thoughts
With tears.

PART THREE

LEANNAIN (LOVERS)

M ost of his life was marked by his loves. Some of them temporary, some long lasting. All were loved by him, many left marks on him, but none could tame him by their definition. Love to him was different.

Some loved loving him, some hated loving him. He loved loving them all. I learned over the years that the difference hurt him as much as it hurt them; filled him as much as it filled them. His concepts of family and life fed into his concept of love, but romantic love went beyond that. He, like Heinlein, sought after *grokking* with those he loved. One might even say to *grok* became a god to him.

For better or worse.

RAIN II

Tears aren't always bad.
They show that you are alive, that you still feel.
Sometimes waiting in the spring rain
They come unexpectedly.
Remembering other spring rain,
I think of ones we spent together.
When was it: eight, ten years ago?
No, it must have been only this morning that…
We slept in, neither of us wanting
To let the moment, or each other, go.
We made love, you giving me you,
Me giving you more than I thought possible.
    In the afternoon you left, and I,
    In quiet desperation, tried to hold onto the time
    We had spent together.
The rain ushered in the night
And all that was left was your perfume to fill the
room.
Spring,
    Your perfume,
        And the rain.

JAZZ:
MONTEREY BAR AND GRILL

When Sunny Gets Blue. The Monterrey Jazz Trio playing on a Friday night, this 31st day of January, 1992. My anthem to Caren (with a C), the love of my life. I had waited and carried with me through a lifeteime a need, defined by a hunger that remained a daily and undeniable emptiness within my inner being. Then she came into my life, filled it with her love, an unbelievable passion, and a tenderness and intimacy that I now find it almost unbearable to exist without.

So I stand here, jazz playing in the background, wishing she were here, or that someone else would or could fill the void that has become my legacy since she left; or if not that, at least that I were in Chicago, where the blues, jazz, and the City (with a capital C) can bend my mind and ease the pain, or at least polarize it and leave me with something other than this emptiness.

There are beautiful women round me, the temptation to seek some surcease from the emptiness fills my mind; appealing to not only my prurient interest but also intriguing

in a subtler fashion—an underlying feel of reciprocation that dares me to pursue but brings me face to face with my worst fear: the fear of winning.

—Dannon Maclir

NEXUS

I watch and see,
All around and encompassing,
Couples and lovers
As they say and do little things
Of no import,
Only that, in circumspect,
They have filled one more hour
Within the aching void
With love,
And each,
The other.

THE NEED

I look up and there you are, walking towards me.
Your hair settles around your face and shoulders,
A wild disarray of loveliness,
And my heart quickens to the rhythm of your step.
I look into your eyes and you smile in recognition,
And something else that you try hard to hide.
We talk and laugh,
Each of us enjoying the time spent together.
We hold each other at arms' length
With a feeling that even that may be too close.
I watch you while you study and you feel my glance,
A question in your eyes as you look into mine,
And I answer you through the windows of my soul.
Can you read what lies there, little girl?
Am I so transparent?
I looked away in confusion; a stab of fear
That you've read the answer much too well.
I collect my books and my thoughts and wish you
goodnight;

I touch your eyes with mine once more,
Then walk into the night
Thanking God for time spent with you,
And praying for something more.

—DANNON MACLIR

THE NEED II

I gaze into the depths of warm brown eyes
Amazed that in their depths there lies a secret
Meant only for me.
The message that I send back to you is palpable.
It has a purpose, defined by the hunger
That stirs my blood when you are near;
Redefined by a beginning warmth
That spreads and permeates my body,
Hoping to devour in a blaze of white heat.
I wish to give you me. Again. And again.
I want to fill you up
And erase from your mind and heart,
Other times,
       Other nights,
              Other lovers.
I wish to take you to heights unreachable;
To feel your soft skin rough against mine,
Making for me a feast, my appetite undiminished.
I want to watch your face
And drink in the depths of your passion,

Fill your lips and tongue with mine
And taste your fire.
I want the heady aroma of your body
To assault my senses; intoxicate me to my core.
I want to hear you cry out in the fury of your passion,
Lost in an oblivion of your own creation.
Fill me up.
I will try to give you more than I receive.
But if I fail, and you give me more of you
Than I give you of me, please wait for a while
And I'll take you back to the beginning
And love you once again.

—DANNON MACLIR

AUTUMN AND YOU

We fly,
    Through falling autumn leaves,
        Laughing, dancing, touching,
With the sun dappling the grass
              through the trees.

I see far,
    Then close,
        Wanting you closer.
I kiss the spray of freckles
        That covers the tip
             of your nose;
my reward,
    A smile
        that touches more
Than just your face.

You glow,
    Face flushed,
        You communicated the need,

Making my constant need for you
Flood my every being.
A lingering kiss
and I am filled,
With love, the autumn,
and you.

AMBUSH

I look up,
    and into,
        eyes,
That catch me unaware
            leaving me bare,
               without defense.
Your smile,
    a hesitant invitation,
        leaves me mute.
Words flow,
    but only from my pen,
for I am stricken
    speechless,
By the beauty
    of
        your
            smile.

—Dannon Maclir

LOVE REMEMBERED

I saw the Dead yesterday.
    They brought back memories
Of warm San Franciscan nights,
    Free concerts in the park
With Grace Slick and Airplane
    Telling us to feed our heads.
Beautiful, willowy, you girls with
    Long skirts, bellbottoms, and tie-dyed blouses;
    Flowers everywhere,
    Assaulting the senses;
        The aphrodisiac of youth.
    Me, in my worn-out blue jeans,
        Hair down past my shoulders,
    Peace sign dangling
        From a leather thong
        Around my neck.
    Skinny, scant-beard, tripping,
        Filled with feelings,
                Overflowing.

And Kat,
      With hair like ebony
And eyes to lose oneself in;
            Loving me each time as if it might be our last,
Knowing that someday it would be.
      Making love, not war.
            Taking time to care,
      Sharing the good and bad,
            Believing it would last forever.
The Grateful Dead and Jerry Garcia
            Doing *In the Midnight Hour*
That seemed to run on and on,
                              Endlessly.

      Stars so bright over the Bay Bridge,
            Reaching out together,
                              Touching each one.
Letting down barriers
            Enduring the rite of passage,

Feeling the magick,

      And then into the mystic.

AND YOU BECOME MY QUEEN AND I, YOUR KING

Child of the night with tender eyes
Fill me up with your song
And I will play you mine,
Minstrelsy to stay your tears,
Madrigals to ease your pain,
Poetry to steal your heart
And love to keep it safe.

Ron

Dannon MacLir

Thank you for the inspiration for,
To me, you are poetry itself.

FAIRY PRINCESS OF THE LAUGHING WOOD

(ANDREA)

Standing there, Lady fair,
I watched her gaze into the glade

Then on tip-toe, head cocked just so,
She stepped forward, unafraid.

"Raven hair, My Lady fair,
You fill my heart with sunshine dreams;
Naught could enhance your fairy dance
Incarnate beauty midst field and stream.

Blossom rare, Lady fair,
You filled the forest with your smile
Followed after by tinkling laughter
To enchant me for a while.

Standing there, Lady fair,
I am entranced by all you do
And from my eyes there always lies
A kiss meant just for you."

—DANNON MACLIR

HEARTS THIEF: FOR CAREN

Butterflies that year
Wore vivid dress
And she, pale in the early spring sun
That filtered through the curtain lace,
Shamed all mortal things
With the essence of her beauty.
The highlight of her hair
Matched the golden rays
Of that larger sun;
Made for me a feast
On her pillow next to mine
I reached out to touch her;
    Velvet soft,
        Radiant warmth;
Hearts thief.
    I love you

DREAMMARE

Cold air blowing
Nightwind changing
Moonlight dancing
On your face
Two hands touching
One heart leaping
To fill with love
The empty space

And I engraving
On mind and tracing
The love you're giving
That fills my cup
Then sunlight filtering
Through window-lacing
On my eyes whispering
To wake me up

SEANNCHAI

Reality waking
As I lay dying
And you lie smiling
Mendacity its evil grin
Heart pounding heaving
As I watch you leaving
And from that grieving
Emptiness once again.

—RON ROGERS

REMEMBER

Gaze back through time
To castle wall
And stare into my eyes;
Changing colors, shifting moods
That tease you, taunt you,
Tantalize.
Until I remove
From your blind eyes
The cloth of time
So you will see
The memory of
That other time
When I touched you
And you touched me.

Remember.

—DANNON MACLIR

PART FOUR

DRAIOCHTA (MAGICK)

We were brought up touched by the whimsy through his guiding hand. Our Celtic heritage (Irish-Scotch-Welsh, God bless us) was important to him because it opened doors to the world of the *sidhe* and the sorcery of a good book. Though he enjoyed introducing us to the magical world of our imaginations, he *poured* it into his youngest daughter and her children. I know she is grateful, and I know the magick—though spurious—is real.

At some point, he felt that magick had left him, but we know the truth. He *is* magick.

MAGICK, by Heather Rhiannon Rogers

When I was just a small child, he told me that we were different, not like everyone else. Even then, as small as I was, I knew it was true. He said that long ago our ancestors had

bred with the fairy folk, and that magick still flowed through our veins. We possessed something rare, something special, a gift that cannot be undone or tamed. Indeed I was different; but it was because he was different, not like the rest. He showed me it was a blessing not a curse to be different, that we must embrace it and walk in its strength, not succumb to the temptation or pressure to be "normal" because we were anything but. We were meant to stand apart, to reach for the things that others had missed, and to take the roads that others had overlooked or simply feared to tread.

I was gifted by the gods with this man as my father, my greatest teacher, and my lifelong best-friend. If you saw him, you'd never guess that he is the living embodiment of Peter Pan. He simply does not age like everyone else, and you'd definitely never guess his true age correctly. He was the age of most of my peers' grandparents, but looked decades younger and had a way of captivating your imagination as only children can do—keeping him younger than most.

Anything was possible when I was with him and everything was as real as our world's dictation of reality goes. We lived in another world, possibly even another dimension where our magick was unhindered by ignorant judgment or biased critique. Neverland was our home where he told me that I'd never be older than five and that he'd always remain ten; that our adventures could continue and never would end.

He read me stories and poetry—Kipling, Wilde, Tolkien, even some of his own. He instilled in me the power that words could hold, especially when they were told from the depths of the heart. A life-long love affair with literature and writing are my most prized gifts he's given me, along with an insatiable appetite for learning any and everything that I possibly can.

My father is anything but normal, a true magick man. He's made every day of my life an adventure (and yes I'm still five as he is ten). He has taught me almost everything that I know. His biggest lesson is that love is the purest form of magick we will ever know.

DOIRCHE

(DARK)

I don't know where/how to start. There is no beginning and apparently, short of this side of the grave, no ending. I don't write anymore. I cannot feel a line of poetry left in my soul; a word of whimsy, a poignant touch, a feel for the game. It's all there but through a glass darkly. At one time after my demise and fall from grace the words just lay there. Bashed and battered, lying at the bottom of that cliff amid the crags and broken rock they escaped, filled my mind and my pen with eloquence.

Now, I believe, I have died an atheist's death. Nothing on the other side, because there simply is no other side. All that time I felt so empty. There is a vast difference between feeling empty and feeling nothing. I expend energy trying to wipe the dark glass clean so that I can open up again and see my world, that world that I thought was empty, that in reality held so much emotion, so much of me, my last hold on innocence. It caused so much pain but it kept me human. I don't know what I am now but maybe this attempt at writing will open the door.

AUTUMN

Love falls
like quiet leaves
On a windy Autumn day;
Drop,
    and land,
        in swirling profusion;
All colors
        bright and beautiful—
Then fade to brown
          and crumble—
'Til spring and life and love
        come once again.

A walk in the woods today put the above thoughts in my mind. 70 degrees in January, apparently, makes poetry drip from the tongue to fall with the sound of "quiet leaves on a windy Autumn day." Somewhere amongst those leaves lies my heart, as crumbled and crumpled as the oak & maple & ash. I searched diligently but could find only a small clue as to where it may be. Too many miles lie between and I suspect that it is lost forever. It leaves me quite sad. To have it back for a day, I would sacrifice all the days left to me; and that is sad, too.

It is good to feel the winds of Faerie upon one's face, the Sun of Summerland touch one's skin; Magick.

I am the Wolf
I am the Windwalker
I am the Sun Catcher
I am the Rain Maker
I am the Wind
I am the Sun
I am the Rain
I am the Wolf who is the Wind
Who is the Sun
Who is the Rain
We are One from Many
The wolf, the Sun, the Wind, the Rain.
I leave my body
Become the Wolf
Become the Wind
Blow Clouds to the Four Winds
I bring the Wind
Become the Storm that brings the Rain
Become the Rain falling
Become the Wolf
That Shadow Walks
Dark forest paths.
I fall; wet, dripping,
softly, silently,
Become the Wind

Blowing away the Clouds,
Becoming the Sun
I become the Wolf.
We are one.

Much of who I am, what I am,
lies in the words of this chant.

WINTERWOLF

Winter night;
The wolf walks,
        stalks,
            cries,
Under frozen silver moon.
On grey-white coat
snowflakes,
        falling softly,
Counterpoint
To cold within.
Journey starting,
Never-ending,
    Seeking
        solitary
            heart,
    Calling.
        Come into
            the wind.
    Come home.

NIGHT KISS

City night
And the muted sounds
Drift
Touching empty rooms
Where memories
Stand waiting
To be reborn

Soft shadows
Listen
In quiet solitude
As the garish sound
Of a neon light
Plays across
The gently blushing
Breeze
And falls silently
Into the summer
Warm

—RON ROGERS

UNBELIEVER

Pariah;
Unclean gestation
Waiting its hour to be born,
It cringes in abject evil.
'Tis misshapen, ugly spawn,
A twisted, gnarled, daemon thing.

Cast not
Into the empty eyes
Strayed souls
Bewailing ancient wrongs;
Deeds conceived in darkest night
That rend and wound and scar the soul.

And one, bereft of all beliefs,
Stares into orbs that petrify;
Turning mortal souls

To standing stone,
And feeling nothing
Is left

       alone.

—DANNON MACLIR

NIGHT THIEF

It comes so;
The insidious grey;
    A cold malignant fog
That bores its evil bit
    Into an open soul.
Driving deep;
    It pierces;
Entering that inner sanctum
    Where dwells
The endless spirit.
Venom drips;
    A dirty, yellow wash,
Conjured from cauldrons,
    Stygian black,
Tended by
    Ancient hags
With eyes devoid
    of souls;
An emptiness that devours.

Endless hunger;
    Thief that stalks the night
To steal all light,
    And souls immortal,
To feed and fill
    Its waiting maw
With fools that dare
        The
        Night.

—DANNON MACLIR

ENCHANTMENT

For the great Gaels of Ireland
Are the men that God made mad,
For all their wars are merry
and all their songs are sad.

—G. K. CHESTERTON

The hills that stand distant in the haze,
The wind that beckons through russet hair,
Pulling strings deep within the hidden heart
Down a road who knows where.

Of fabled journey to Netherland
Of mystic hero and epic breed,
Facing life with fire and a fighting hand;
Fulfilling the lusty berserk's need.

From a sunrise drenched in a warriors blood
To sunset impassioned in a maiden's eyes;
From a summer's song, a life well spent
To winter rain as death draws nigh.

—RON ROGERS

BROTHER SUN, SISTER WIND

The Sun and the Wind,
In unison,
Caress the trees
Gently, with tender touch,
As they embrace every leaf.
Like the strings of a mandolin,
They play Autumn's song upon
The eloquent instruments
Of Mother Earth.
Both scatter and sparkle
Upon the surface of the lake;
The breeze sculpting patterns
That the Sun may shine its radiance
And make the morning brilliant
With its rays
As they danced upon the music of the wind.

—DANNON MACLIR

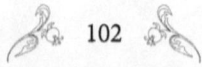

THE HEALING

Rain.
Pitter patter, falling softly.
Gentle caress,
Tender touch,
Enveloping those
torn and bloody.
Wresting pain and anger
From beleaguered hearts
Until
Tears fall, and then
Silence
And the night.

—RON ROGERS

BLESSED

Green buds
&
Grey bark;
Beauty
of
the
coming
spring…
Portents of love's inception
&
the
All-spiritual
One.
I Search,
And while wondering,
Feel
The Magick in all things;
I
am
blessed.

THE HAVE-BEENS

I sat in my window tonight and, while listening to Clannad, started cleaning my two swords. The wind and the night have a chill to it and, for just a moment, I thought I felt the magick. Whether it was real or just a residue of something that I have lost, I can't be sure. I do know that it is almost 11:00 pm and whatever it was pushed me out the door, pen and notebook in hand, to wind up writing this in a booth at Denny's.

How many poems and how much prose have I sat in this place and written? I don't have a clue, but the numbers are significant. The magick has, or is in the process, of slipping away. It wasn't here long enough to leave that melancholy Celtic Twilight mood that used to be such a part of me. Is it better to exist in bland contentment and not feel all the highs and lows or is my loss greater than even I imagine? I used to love walking in the chill damp air and feel the spray of rain across my face as the night took me in its arms and held me close and whispered to me, "Come into the Wind, Come Home." Now I feel the wind and rain but it no longer pulls me into the night. Or not enough…not until tonight.

So, here I sit, thinking it's another false alarm but then again hoping that I can put together one small piece of poetry that I deem worth keeping.

"I close my eyes to dreaming, only
long enough to dream."

I was listening to my Caren tape this afternoon while working and was struck by the depth of my feelings for her still. I still replay might-have-beens, should-have-beens, would-have-beens, but it all still comes back to the same end… she's gone. She shouldn't be. She should be curled up in my arms, head lying on my chest, sharing every breath I take. Velvet soft, radiant warmth, I love you. It's funny that I can write about it now and not feel the pain but still want her with every bit of my being. I just wish I could see her for one hour and talk to her and watch the sunlight play in her hair and have her look at me for just that short time like she once did. Then a hug goodbye and feel her tremble in my arms as she did on the first night we met. Then walk out the door forever. That would be enough.

"…but because he has seen, darkly with a child's eyes, how the gods move with the winds and speak with the sea and sleep with the gentle herbs; and how God Himself is the sum of all that is on the face of the lovely earth. Magick is the door through which mortal man may sometimes step to find the gates in the Hollow Hills, and let himself through into the halls of that other world."

—MARY STEWART

thus, the root of what small magick I may have acquired. The hills, the wind, the lovely leaf-strewn places; the sun falling ever gentle on my face. Drawing magick from the scent of pines, the dry pungent smell of fallen autumn leaves, the white tail deer with its pensive stare through the branches of winter trees. These are what magick holds and what holds magick to me. Like Merlin, I wait, for it comes in its own time and I am but its vessel to be filled by the whim of the God.

-- ∞ --

I went to the woods. it was raining when I entered but after a half hour or so it started snowing, big flakes, and the world turned. Rain, snow, fog, those quiet breathless moments at dawn and even more so at dusk, those times when our world touches the other world, this was my world for two hours.

All greatness of all men die; are interred with their bones and become food for worms. A little time of mourning; a memory, bittersweet and melancholy, then a dwindling into nothingness.

My father was such a man to remember. The world should know the stuff of such as he was made. But only I make the pilgrimage to his grave and shed a tear in his honor. Only my good friend, Bill Linne, shares my loss and pain, but that is enough.

My father was a saunterer. To watch him walk, hands in pockets, seemingly without a care in the world, was a delight; a touch of whimsy, a half smile or cocky grin to light the way. The word saunter is…beautifully derived from "idle people who roved about the country in the Middle Ages and asked charity, under the pretense of going 'a la Sainte Terre' (to the Holy Land), till the children exclaimed, 'There goes a Saint Terre!' A Holylander. A Saunterer."

The words above from Henry David Thoreau's essay, *Walking*. He further states, "We should go forth on the shortest walks, perchance, in the spirit of undying adventure, never to return—prepared to send back our embalmed hearts only as relics to our desolate kingdoms. If you are ready to leave father & mother, and brother & sister, and wife & child & friends, and never see them again; if you have paid your debts, made your will, and settled all your affairs, and are a free man, then you are ready for a walk."

To saunter.

My father was a man who, when he walked, became poetry that bespoke of leaves falling, autumn colors rife, of a sadness—a melancholy—of sere wintry winds; but, most of all, an unnegotiable & unequivocal freedom.

He sauntered.

A "Sainte Terre" in search of whatever Holy Land that resided within his being. Looking into my mind, I see him even now and pray that he found the way.

I saunter, too.

PART FIVE

SEANNCHAI (STORYTELLER)

Every story has a heartache, and the Poet's heartache was too often family. But that doesn't mean life and goodness never came from it. He is to this day estranged from his daughter Tina, but she was able to see the beauty in this part of his life. What did it mean to her that he was always a man of words? Let her tell you in her own.

STORYTELLER, by Tina Brison

I have always believed in the magick of stories. Without him, the gift of stories would not be mine. Not only did he fill my childhood with the sound of his voice reading the works of others (I can still hear the capital "T" in his voice when he spoke of The Trilogy—The Lord of the Rings), but with tales and poems of his own making.

His stories were often romantic, sometimes sad, but always magical. He told the kinds of tales that pull at one's heart and give the imagination wings to soar. His fantastical worlds held more than child-like wonder; they held adult wonder, something hard to come by for anyone over the age of twenty. He never lost that wonder, and he never lost the need to share it with others.

As I got older, he was more likely to hand me pages to read than to tell the story himself, and I did so gladly, always eager for the wizardry of his words.

Because he shared his love of words with me, my life has been on a trajectory of words from birth. His love of books and writing made them such an integral part of my life that it was a natural extension of myself to become a writer. He told stories like they were air, and as I grew up, they became air to me, too.

I hope his stories hold the same magick for you.

For me, the bard in every tale has his face.

DUBLIN TOWN

I wonder what they're doing
Tonight in Dublin town.
Does the gang still think of me
And wish that I were still around?
Does each of them remember
Tears of laughter, tears of pain,
And how we helped each other?
Does the love we shared remain?
Do Sean and Meg and Alastair
Remember me in fond regards,
How when we were but wee children
We played and laughed in the old courtyard?
And how Megan's Grandma, visage grim,
Would reprimand us for our foolish play
And we in somber, solemn state
Fell to fits of laughter when she went away!
And later, when we had grown
Drinking beer on Meg's front lawn,
My young heart was torn
When Meg professed her love for Sean.
Alastair and I got drunk that night,

For he loved sweet Megan, too;
Her fiery hair and sea blue eyes
would capture any of you.
My broken heart, still filled with love
Could not mend or stand the pain
To watch love's radiance shine for them
While I stood in the falling rain.
That's really why I left, you know,
Went to Shannon till it turned cold
Then shipped out on a freighter.
It was on their wedding day, I'm told.
Been fifteen years or more
Since I've seen sweet Ireland's shore,
But I still remember lovely Megan
Standing by her front porch door.

With tears and anquish on her face,
She gave me one last kiss goodbye
and said, "I love you, too,"
And so that she could not see my cry,
I turned and ran, not looking back,
Her crying ringing in my ears
And I've not been back again,
Although it's been most fifteen years.
Now I walk memory's cobbled streets
Trying to put it all behind,
But I still think of Dublin Town
With thoughts of Meg on my mind.

CHANT RANN

He approached the old man
With a drunken leer
Smelling like a brewery
From the whiskey, wine, and beer.
He said, "I've seen ye here before, old man,
Putting on such airs,
you think you're something special
But no one really cares."
The old man at first said nothing,
Just stared into the flames;
A last bastion from the winter's cold
Chilling body, soul, and brain.
Then he turned and faced the wreck
That once had been a man
And said, "My friend I am in need,
Help me if you can."
The sot was taken quite aback
At the old man's plea
And a feeling of something lost
Seemed to plague his memory.

He tried to focus bleary eyes
To see the old man's face,
But where a countenance should have been
Only shadows filled the space.
As he looked he felt a chill,
Tried desperately to reach the light
And from the old man turned to run
But something held him in the night.
"You'd not be leavin' lad,
With the wind so through the trees,
And be feeling the rain upon your face,
How it can tantalize and tease.
Does remind of another time
When looking into the fire,
I saw warriors singing battle songs
In the glory that was Eire."

Then from his ragged, ratty coat
Made from a canvas tarp,
The old man bowed and drew from it
An ancient, battered harp.
Lovingly he touched it,
Took it gently in his hand
And with one note midst wind and rain
The fiery flames were fanned.
The drunk, in awe, stood silently
And as the rain turned to pelting snow,

The old man stripped down to the waist
And in stature seemed to grow.
Then he laid his fingers, nimble quick
Upon the ancient strings
And as the music mesmerized,
He lifted up his voice to sing:

"Waves beat on ancient strand
Ceremonial drums that fill the night
And through it all, warriors stalk;
Souls of *was* in mystic flight.
Gods of discord rant and cry,
Adding to the cacophony
As battle lines are being drawn
On sandy shores by Irish sea.
Then from the ranks of Clan McDonal,
Amid the growing din and hue,
A man with coat of many colors
And battered harp strode into view.
With practiced finger, he strummed a note,
As if giving prelude to what would be,
Then lifted his voice in arcane chant
To caress and coax both strand and sea.
Then, magically, the day grew darker,
Black clouds and thunder filled the sky.
Then streaks of lightning and gale-force winds
Brought forth from Kerry Clan a cry.

Waves rose up, dashed rock and shoal,
Fear rampant ran through rank and file.
With growing fury the minstrel played
And the enemy host he did beguile.
His chant in crescendo filled the air
In one last burst, impassioned plea,
'Kerry Clan, begone and cease
This foolish game you play with me.'
And, as if an omen, lightning struck
In angry rage between the host
And the fury of its rage
Seemed to inundate the coast.
Under the dark forbidding gloom
Kerry faces blanched in fear
At this ancient apparition
That loomed in umbral darkness there.
Then one brave warrior of Kerry Clan
Stepped forth with outstretched, empty arms
And said, 'I know not how to stop or stay
The spell you weave with music's charms.
Perhaps there is a better way to find surcease,
To mend the wounds that now abide
Between Clan McDonal and Kerry Clan,
To live together side by side.'
The minstrel stood there silently
Then to the Kerry host's dismay,
He once again took up his harp
But a different song began to play.

It brought with it the clarity
And beauty of an Autumn morn
And in the hearts of all who heard,
Peace and love again were born.
Warriors cast down sword and spear
And as the troubadour played his air,
They gazed across the sunlit sand
At their brothers waiting there.

The bard lifted up his voice in strength
And said, 'From this day forward,
Hearts of Kerry, I wish you well.
May peace between us be our pledge;
May brotherhood between us live,
And should my brother be in need
All I have to him I'll give.
And in dark times of wind and rain
When clouds of gloom fill sky above,
Remember the magick of my song
And fill your hearts with peace and love.'
Then the minstrel turned toward the sea,
Lifted up his voice once more
And cried, 'My father, take me now
From this Irish sand and shore.'
Waves rose up to catch the shoals,
Washed up to mark the minstrel's way.
Then, silently, with measured tread,
He walked into the ocean spray.

The host, in somber quietude,
Gave silent homage, every man
To the magick minstrel who
Had saved the brotherhood of the Clans.
Together they held a victory feast,
A feast of love to rule the land,
And gave special thanks to the coming
of the magick minstrel man."

Thus, with bowed head, the tale was ended
And as snow turned back into rain,
A warm wind blew bringing with it
A smell of ocean to the drunkard's brain.
As he shook his head in wonder,
The old man began to speak once more.
He said, "Come, lad, and walk with me,
Back to ancient Ireland's shore."

Then the Bard held out his hand.
The drunk knelt to one knee
And heard the old man say, "My friend,
As now I am, so you will be."
With that they walked into the night,
Ocean tang still in the air,
To ancient Emerald Isle of Light
and the magick waiting there.

—RON ROGERS

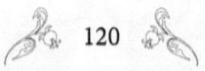

*"I looked and there before
me was a pale horse! Its
rider was named death…"*

—REVELATION 6:8

THE IMMORTAL

Images flit in shades of grey,
Illusions capture and memories strain;
Wild heart beating in muffled tones
To the muted pounding in my brain.

Shadowed memories fill the mind,
Faded visions beyond recall
Wending down a well-worn path
To come to rest at garden wall.

Siege machines in battle lines
Drawn up to breach my prison gate,
I crouch in fear and black despair
As spectral demons watch and wait.

And then he comes, my old friend.
Behold! His steed a ghostly pale
And with mystic sign and arcane spell
He frees me from my earthly jail.

Then I mount, helped by his hand;
He laughs and speaks in joyous glee,
"Welcome once again, my friend,
come and spend some time with me."

The portal for my immortal soul
Transporting me from sleep into the dawn
Opens wide and beckons me
As from this world I'll soon be gone.

And I will rise, be born again;
Be cast into a future state
Where I will battle dark once more
And dare to face my final fate.

Then off upon the spirit wind
That Gods and dreamers were born to ride,
'Midst lightning, thunder, and the gale
With death, my brother, at my side.

—DANNON MACLIR

DEATH SONG

IT comes, this time,
                    every year.
Leaves change, burst into
                    breath-taking beauty,
Then die.
It is but a short time,
And then the winter rains
                    begin.

AFTERTHOUGHT

I stop, at times, inopportune,
Without volition of my own,
And between memories, bittersweet
I recall other loves and other lovers—
Some remembered well, others not at all—
Each deserving of something more.
But now and then, even then, each has touched me,
Filled me for at least a night; others nightly.
Some with a blaze of white-hot heat,
Consuming me with a fire of my own creation,
Kindled by caresses, hot and sweet,
And lips and tongue to tantalize;
A work of art, they become complete
Only when I hear them cry out,

       The little death;

        Passion spent.

DRAIOCHT SEANACHAI

I

Up to her, he strode
As she stood there by the sea
And said, "My bonnie, blue-eyed lass,
Have a walk with me."
She looked at him with some disdain,
Her lips drawn into a frown,
Then tossed her curls into the air
And turned herself around.
"I'll have naught to do with such a fool
That dreams his life away.
So save your verse and silvery tongue,
I'll not be led astray."
With eyes cast down he made no move,
Dejection on him like a cloak,
And as she made to walk away,
These few words he spoke:
"I cannot offer mansions vast

Or castles by the sea,
I know not where I'll lay my head
But as sure as the Old Gods live and breathe
Under summer sky and wintery sea,
The web is cast, the fates are sealed,
One day you'll come to me."
She watched him as he walked away,
The sea wind whipping his cloak and hair
And she felt a tug within her breast
From feelings she had not known were there
And thought, "I mustn't show him how I feel
For soon I know he will be gone
Like the fairy folk of yore,
Leannan sidhe and leprechaun."

II

The falling leaves of Autumn
Brought rampant colors to fill the air
Filling every wayward gypsy soul
With poetry and words to share.
With every other vagabond,
The whimsey and the wanderlust
And naught could stay their wandering feet
Nor break the age-old trust.
To seek the ancient winding roads
Leaf-strewn, dim, and sere

With the wind blowing through the trees
And a sadness in the air.
So upon a night with silver moon
In full regalia beaming down,
It touched the heads of the gathering
And become for them a magick crown.
It blessed them with its arcane glow
As they danced within the fairy ring,
Then one above the others
Lifted up his voice to sing:

"Mother Goddess, Father, Son,
We pray you hear our plea!
Grant us beauty in our every words
That everyone may see
All the beauties of the world
Below us and above,
To share our words with those who care
To live in peace and love."
Then from the ring of fairy kind
Around those waiting there,
The gentle folk were cast in light
That shone on them so fair.
The air was filled with haunting sound,
Sweet melody to warm the night,
And give a gift of gentle speech
To use for good to hold the light.

III

So he gave his love to verse and rhyme
And through all the forty years gone by,
He'd seen her only one more time.
It was in a bookstore, Dark & Drear
In oldest Dublin Town,
Someone thrust a book at him
As he'd turned around.
It was his latest book of verse
Laid bare for him to see
And he'd read the title page out loud,
"My Fair Lady of the Sea."
And so it was, as he looked up
Into trembling smile and eyes of blue,
With gentle hand she touched his cheek
And said, "I can't believe it's you."
As she took her hand away
It seemed to catch the light.
Her finger held a wedding ring
Gold and diamond bright.
She looked at him with tear-filled eyes,
Shudders wracked her anguished frame,
"Sean, you said to you I'd come
And God, I wish I'd came.
But I was young and headstrong then,
Too proud to see my greed.
Blind to hide my love from you

When it's you I need."
He'd stood there in the silence,
Her head upon his chest,
Then tilted up her chin
And with his lips he pressed
Her lips as sweet as honey,
Then pulled himself away.
"I've loved you as life itself,"
He said, "but can't lead you astray."
He'd taken the book from her hand
And from the pocket of his coat,
He took a pen to cover page
And on that page he wrote:

As long as there is earth below
And sun and moon above,
My Fair Lady of the Sea
Will be my only love.

He returned the book of verse,
Touched her cheek once more,
Then turned from her stricken stare
And walked out through the door.

-- ∞ --

So now he sat in winter sun
That warmed the day and filled the lea

And thought, "All I need is flowers budding
To make it seem like spring to me."
With that, he closed his eyes to nap
And on his knees a book he propped.
Then he smiled, his breathing slowed
And then, at last, it stopped.

IV

The years had gone by quickly,
The days had come and gone.
She went back to her husband
But her heart belonged to Sean.
She kept him there for quiet times
Knowing how her foolish pride
Had kept him from her side.
'Twas late in November month
In the year of sixty-five,
Her husband James had a stroke
And the next day he died.
She spent a year in mourning,
"Twas proper," the people said,
"For a good and proper wife
To give honor to the dead."
Then her black dress she boxed away
And with it all her past.
She caught a train to Dublin Town
Where she had seen him last.

She hastened to the bookstore
Hoping by some chance she'd find
A way to reach the man she loved
And put the past behind.

V

The bell above the bookstore door
Made silvery sounds as she walked in.
She approached the grey-haired clerk
Wondering how she should begin.
Before she could say a word,
He smiled and reached out his hand
And said, "I'd know you anywhere,
You're where it all began."
She thought, "My God, he's crazy,"
and turned at once to leave,
But before she could reach the door
He had her by the sleeve.
He said, "My dear, I'm sorry,
I've given you quite a fright,
For if you're not Sean's Lady of the Sea,
Then I guess you have the right
To think my actions strange indeed
And to Bedlam be interred.
But if you are the Lady of the Sea
Then please let me be heard."
He stepped behind the counter,

Took the measure of her heart,
Then said with downcast eyes,
"I know not where to start."
Her mind was filled with quiet
As she listened to what was said.
"Start from the beginning."
He said, "Your Sean is dead.
He'd been staying out at me farm
Seeing no one at all,
Avoiding contact with the world
Unless I came to call.
We talked of many things, we did
Through many a winter's eve
And stoically through it all,
For you, I watched him grieve.
You were his inspiration,
Twas you who spurred him on.
Twas you he wrote his verses for
And now, God bless, he's gone."
The old man took his handkerchief
And wiped away a tear,
Raised his hand to ward her off
As she attempted to draw near.
He reached under the counter
And pulled from it a sack.
Then handed it to her
And leaned his body back.
"I was the one that found him

In a rare snow and cold as sin,
Dressed as if the summer's warmth
Had somehow come again.
He lay propped up to an oak
And on his frozen knee,
A copy of his book of verse,
My Lady of the Sea.
This is all I have for you,
Now by God I wish you'd go.
He's buried in Glasnevin.
I guess that he'd want you to know."

VI

The sky was grey and blustery cold
The wind a howling, living thing,
But within the graveyard by his grave
Deep within the fairy ring,
A man with coat of many colors
For the wee folk his harp did play,
And within that magick circle
All was cheerful, bright, and gay.
Almost, the music seemed to die,
As he watched the Wee Folk slip away.
Then, one turned to him and said,
"Sean, she comes. We cannot stay."

'twas no trouble to find his grave.
it lay within a grove of trees—
blackthorn, ash, and father oak—
the leaves stirring with the breeze.
they had warned her that his stone
seemed old and worn before its time
and on it his only epitaph
were eight lines of verse and rhyme.
as she stepped into the grove of trees
the wind abated, caught its breath,
and seemed to wait in silent wonder
within this hallowed place of death.
the stone was ancient, out of time,
a battered Celtic Cross,
and as she stared amidst glade and grave
it seemed to magnify her loss.
then cold wind blew her tears to ice
as she reached his final place of rest.
she read the verse upon the stone
it went like a knife into her breast.

I cannot offer mansions vast
Or castles by the sea.
I know not where I'll lay my head
Or what the morrow hold for me.
But surely as the old gods live and breathe

under summer sky and wintery sea,
The web is cast, the fates are sealed.
One day you'll come to me.

It had been two score years and more
Since those words she'd heard him say.
Now here they were to haunt her soul
At how she'd let him walk away.
So she knelt before the stone
Placed there her cheek in silent stark
And said, "Sean, I cannot leave you here
All alone in the cold and dark.
And there she lay her body upon his grave
As down her cheek ran frozen tears,
Wishing that there was a way
To gain back all the years.
Then through the high and lofty trees
A sunbeam filtered down
And touched the aged lines of her face
And spread healing warmth around.
It grew around her like a spell
Cast to bring an early spring.
High up within the Father Oak,
A meadowlark began to sing.
She shrugged out of her winter coat,
Made for her head a pillow,

For the warmth had made her drowsy
And spring breeze had made her mellow.
As she drifted off to sleep,
Her mind and body growing numb,
She said, "Sean, I'm sorry that I'm late.
But, ye know, I've finally come."

THE POETRY MAN

Once there was a Poetry Man
Who was guide by the light,
Who carried the torch of chivalry,
Of God and truth and right.
But somewhere he lost connexions
Ran out of songs to play,
And now his fears have cost him tears
And now he lives as one who's dead
And dies a little more each day.

Around his neck, he wears the ring,
It says *Class of '65*;
He won it in a waking dream
But it's better that he never were alive
Than pay the price that he now pays,
For in his brain all that remains
Is a land, forlorn and stark,
And on his soul the dismal mark
Of the ring and its bloody stain.

It took him on a long and winding journey,
Fraught with burden like a blight,
Filled with demons and the one Dark Lord,
Becoming one with the spectral night.
Tempted twice by evil, lured on by faith
To mend his heart and ease the pain,
While in their lair with golden hair
With words and spells they laid him bare
And took from him all that he had gained.

In anger he shook his fist,
In rage he cried out his disdain,
"Altho' my eyes run tears of blood
And see nothing through the blood but rain,
I'm still the warrior, the Poetry Man,
Light and good lie within me still,
and in the dark still lies a spark,
In my breast my heart beats strong,
And I'll not use the ring for ill."

And down from his dark throne
With a howl of fury the Dark Lord came.
The warrior stood there silently,
Whispering the music of her name.
And with it her song,
Just a memory in his mind's eye,
and like an animal haltered,

So the Dark Lord faltered;
Watched the song of love enfold him,
Watched with love the Dark Lord die.

From his neck he took the ring,
The burden carried, finally gone.
But he needs must think of her once more,
yet memory fades just like the dawn.
With tears streaming down his face,
The Poet turned and walked away.
It was her he was thinking of and how he'd lost her love,
And his soul in darkness dwells
And will until dying day.

—DANNON MACLIR

ENDING?

There are lines of poetry & prose, and lines within lines, that, by turns, enlighten us, ensnare us, empower us, and devastate us; sorrow, laughter, poignancy, melancholy, happiness; pain. I will try to remember to add these words that touch me in that private room that we keep for ourselves only, to these pages. After all, have I not lived by the principles that I learned in those special tomes and do they not lay me bare unto myself so that I may articulate who and what and where I am and bring to reality what I feel and believe?

> "… I've got a gray and ragged
>   brother in my breast—
> that's a fact. Back of Chicago the open
> field—long trains go west, too—in
> the silence. Don't fret love.
> I'll come out all right."

—*EVENING SONG*, BY SHERWOOD ANDERSON

EPILOGUE

OIDHREACHT

(LEGACY)

Every story has an ending, and the Poet's ending is still in play. What a shame it would be if it came and went and none were the wiser, the better, the clearer about life for it. I hope these stories and poems crafted in you a desire to make everything—family, life, love, magick, and, yes, storytelling—a part of who you are.

Then pass it on.

This isn't so much about a man as it is about a philosophy, one that has helped to shape my understanding of the world, of humanity, even of God. I'm richer for it. Perhaps you are, too. And maybe—just maybe—you'll find your own voice, and the air will be filled with your storytelling.

SEANNCHAI

The cold smell of potato mould, the squelch and slap
Of soggy peat, the curt cuts of an edge
Through living roots awaken in my head.
But I've no spade to follow men like them.

Between my finger and my thumb
The squat pen rests.
I'll dig with it.

—FROM "DIGGING," BY SEAMUS HEANEY